From BLACK

WALL STREET

to ALLENSWORTH

HEDREICH NICHOLS with KELISA WING

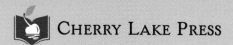
CHERRY LAKE PRESS

Published in the United States of America by Cherry Lake Publishing Group
Ann Arbor, Michigan
www.cherrylakepublishing.com

Reading Adviser: Beth Walker Gambro, MS, Ed., Reading Consultant, Yorkville, IL
Content Adviser: Kelisa Wing
Book Design and Cover Art: Felicia Macheske

Photo Credits: © trevor kittelty/Shutterstock.com, 5; © Bildagentur Zoonar GmbH/Shutterstock.com, 7; © Gill Copeland/ Shutterstock.com, 9; Library of Congress, George Grantham Bain Collection, Control No: 2014688320, 11; Library of Congress, Photo by Russell Lee, Control No: 2017788995, 13; © GreenPimp/iStock.com, 15; © RGB Ventures/SuperStock/Alamy Stock Photo, 17; © Stan Reese/Shutterstock.com, 19; © Icom Images/Alamy Stock Photo, 21; © Zack Frank/Shutterstock.com, 23; © Everett Collection/Shutterstock, 25; © Vineyard Perspective/Shutterstock.com, 27; U.S. National Archives, ARC 2794752. RG 302, public domain, www.flickr.com/photos/inshaw/3902809966/in/album-72157600532705947/, 29; © wavebreakmedia/ Shutterstock.com, 30

Graphics Throughout: © debra hughes/Shutterstock.com; © Galyna_P/Shutterstock.com

Library of Congress Cataloging-in-Publication Data

Names: Nichols, Hedreich, author. | Wing, Kelisa, author.
Title: From Black Wall Street to Allensworth / by Hedreich Nichols and Kelisa Wing.
Description: Ann Arbor, Michigan : Cherry Lake Publishing, [2022] | Series: Racial justice in America: excellence and achievement | Audience: Grades 7-9 | Summary: "Students will learn more about America's thriving Black communities, from Tulsa's Black Wall Street to Allensworth, California. These towns and neighborhoods are often ignored in discussions on Black America and their success was often met with resistance—often violent resistance. This book illuminates the achievement and culture of these communities, while exploring racism in a comprehensive, honest, and age-appropriate way. Developed in conjunction with educator, advocate, and author Kelisa Wing to reach children of all races and encourage them to approach our history with open eyes and minds. Books include 21st Century Skills and content, activities created by Wing, table of contents, glossary, index, author biography, sidebars, and educational matter" —Provided by publisher.
Identifiers: LCCN 2021047061 | ISBN 9781534199347 (hardcover) | ISBN 9781668900482 (paperback) | ISBN 9781668906248 (ebook) | ISBN 9781668901922 (pdf)
Subjects: LCSH: African Americans—United States—Economic conditions—Juvenile literature. | African Americans—United States--Social conditions—20th century—Juvenile literature. | African American neighborhoods—History—Juvenile literature. | United States—Race relations—History—20th century—Juvenile literature. | Successful people—United States—Juvenile literature.
Classification: LCC E185.8 .N53 2021 | DDC 305.896/073—dc23
LC record available at https://lccn.loc.gov/2021047061

Cherry Lake Publishing Group would like to acknowledge the work of the Partnership for 21st Century Learning, a Network of Battelle for Kids. Please visit http://www.battelleforkids.org/networks/p21 for more information.

Printed in the United States of America
Corporate Graphics

Hedreich Nichols, author, educator, and host of the YouTube series on equity #SmallBites, is a retired Grammy-nominated singer-songwriter turned EdTech teacher who uses her experience as a "one Black friend" to help others understand race, equity, and how to celebrate diversity. When not educating and advocating, she enjoys making music with her son, multi-instrumentalist @SwissChrisOnBass.

Kelisa Wing honorably served in the U.S. Army and has been an educator for 14 years. She is the author of *Promises and Possibilities: Dismantling the School to Prison Pipeline*, *If I Could: Lessons for Navigating an Unjust World*, and *Weeds & Seeds: How to Stay Positive in the Midst of Life's Storms*. She speaks both nationally and internationally about discipline reform, equity, and student engagement. Kelisa lives in Northern Virginia with her husband and two children.

Untold Stories of Black Wealth

When we read about Black history, we usually read about moments connected with enslavement and oppression, or protests and civil rights. The best-known heroes are people like Martin Luther King Jr. or Harriet Tubman and others connected with those great and important struggles for freedom.

What our history books don't usually cover are stories of wealth and success in the Black community. Despite all the challenges Black Americans have faced, there have been many entrepreneurs, politicians, inventors, academicians, and business owners whose achievements and stories are largely unknown.

In this book, you will learn about some of those stories and communities.

Black Wealth in Africa

In the years before Europeans began colonizing nations, many powerful African civilizations thrived. Advanced civilizations like the Great Zimbabwe, the Mali empire, Egypt, and the kingdoms of Benin and Mutapa were known for architecture, art, mathematics, science, and military achievement. These economic powerhouses were attractive to European traders because of their gold, textiles, and other resources. As colonization spread, European settlers laid claim to African land and resources, and eventually, even some of the people. Colonial trade practices and national civil wars both played roles in the downfall of the great African kingdoms.

Great Mosque of
Djenné, Mali

Before European settlers traveled to Africa, the continent included many great and powerful nations. Europeans kidnapped many Africans to be sold as slaves in the American colonies. When enslavement became illegal after the U.S. Civil War, millions of descendants of the enslaved Africans were freed. However, they were not given money, homes, or land. They had to start over with nothing. Many of the formerly enslaved people didn't survive. Those who did had to figure out how to make something from nothing.

This statue in Zanzibar, Tanzania, commemorates the lives lost to enslavement. Zanzibar is a port city that once played a major role in the enslavement and trafficking of humans.

CHAPTER 1

The Sweet Auburn District, Atlanta, Georgia

One person who was good at making something from nothing was Alonzo Herndon, the first Black millionaire of Atlanta, Georgia. Herndon began his life as a **freedman**. Even though he was the son of his enslaver, he was homeless and penniless. Herndon worked at whatever jobs he could find. He learned to be a barber and eventually owned several barber shops. In 1905 he founded an insurance company. This company, along with the Citizens Trust Bank founded by Herman Perry and his partners, was the financial base of the "Sweet Auburn" community in Atlanta. The Citizens Trust Bank has grown to be the largest federally certified Black financial banking institution in the United States today.

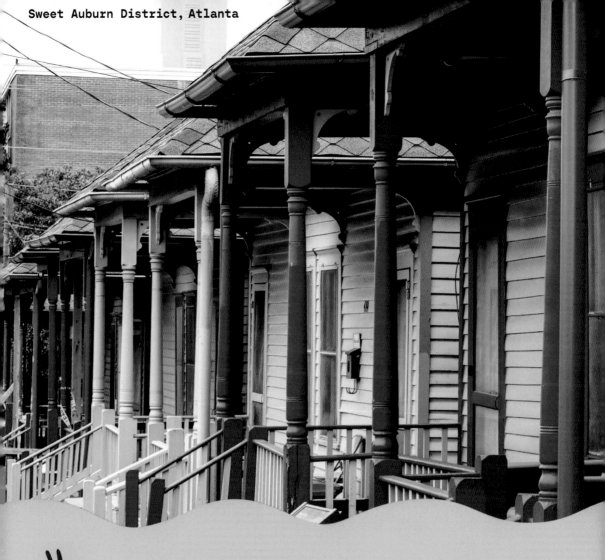

An estimated 4 million enslaved Africans and their descendants were freed when slavery was abolished in the United States. They won their freedom but lost access to food, clean water, and whatever living resources they received as enslaved people. An estimated 1 million of those freed died of starvation, exposure to weather, and illnesses. This little-known U.S. tragedy is exposed and explored in depth by author Jim Downs in *Sick from Freedom*.

In the early 1900s, the Sweet Auburn District was a thriving community that was home to beauty salons, hotels, stores, and many other types of businesses. Famous Black night spots and restaurants were there, as well as the Black newspaper and the civil rights organization the National Association for the Advancement of Colored People (NAACP). The churches in the district were large and well known, including Ebenezer Baptist Church where Dr. Martin Luther King Jr. was pastor.

Today the Auburn Avenue area that was known as the Sweet Auburn District is a protected historic district. People are working to preserve it. You can visit Dr. King's childhood home, the church, and other historical landmarks in the neighborhood virtually or in person.

Black Codes and Segregation

Shortly after the Confederate army lost the Civil War, Southern states created Black Codes, also known as Jim Crow laws. These laws prevented Black people from enjoying many of the freedoms of citizenship. They also restricted where Black people could live or operate businesses. The positive effect of this segregation was that Black resources were concentrated in certain areas of the country.

CHAPTER 2

Bronzeville, Chicago, Illinois

The Bronzeville neighborhood—also known as the Black Belt—on Chicago's South Side was home to more than 250,000 people during its peak in the early to mid-1900s. As Black people moved away from the South in the Great Migration, many came to Chicago. The large city offered Black people the chance to succeed. In Chicago, the man who provided a financial foundation for the community was Jesse Binga. He owned the city's first Black insurance company and bank. The Binga bank helped many business owners to get their start. Those business owners could then hire others, which helped the community's wealth grow.

The Bronzeville community was home to all kinds of people—rich, poor, professionals, tradesmen, writers, filmmakers, and entertainers. Bronzeville was also a place where culture and the arts flourished. Venues like the Savoy Ballroom were said by some to rival the great Apollo Theater in the Harlem area of New York City.

Musicians like Louis Armstrong, Ella Fitzgerald, and Billie Holiday all performed at the Savoy Ballroom.

Some of the greatest names in jazz and gospel music came from Bronzeville. They included Louis Armstrong, Nat "King" Cole, Mahalia Jackson, and Quincy Jones. We still hear their songs today. If you have heard Nat Cole's "The Christmas Song" on your radio or have Michael Jackson's *Thriller* album on your playlist, you've heard famous musicians from the Bronzeville community.

Bronzeville was also an important place for technology and medical science. Black surgeon Daniel Hale Williams performed the first successful documented open-heart surgery there in Provident Hospital.

Most hospitals would not treat Black people. If they did, hospitals gave them only the most basic, or even harmful, standards of care. Also, Black doctors and nurses were not allowed to treat White people. In 1891 Dr. Daniel Hale Williams founded Provident Hospital, the first Black-owned and Black-operated hospital and training school in the United States. It was an important first that served the people of Bronzeville and the nation.

Quincy Jones

Quincy Jones was one of many famous musicians born in Bronzeville. His career spans almost 70 years, perhaps more years than your grandparents have been alive! Jones worked with other famous musicians such as Miles Davis and Aretha Franklin. He also serves as a mentor to popular YouTuber Jacob Collier. Jones has earned four platinum and two gold recordings. He has had top-40 hits in multiple decades. Jones is probably most famous for his work with Michael Jackson on the Grammy Award–winning *Thriller* album, the best-selling album of all time.

CHAPTER 3

The Fourth Avenue District, Birmingham, Alabama

If you think of Birmingham, Alabama, you may think of marches, civil rights protests, and the Ku Klux Klan church bombing that killed four young Black girls. However, Birmingham's Fourth Avenue District was a thriving area and home to retail businesses, theaters, lawyers' offices, and medical practices. By day, food was bought, clothing was tailored, shoes were shined, transport was arranged, and pride was felt for the many accomplishments by and for the Black community. By night, that pride lived on as members of the community sang, danced, and gathered in theaters and concert venues like the Carver Theatre.

Today, the Fourth Avenue Historic District runs for three
blocks in downtown Birmingham.

A.G. Gaston

A. G. Gaston was always an entrepreneur with a vision. It is reported that as a child, he sold rides on his backyard swing in exchange for buttons. As a teenager, he started a funeral insurance business. He became a multimillionaire, owning several profitable businesses such as a construction company, radio stations, a bank, a business college, and a funeral business with locations all over Alabama. Gaston was also a negotiator and a quiet behind-the-scenes civil rights activist. You can read more about Gaston in his memoir, *Green Power: The Successful Way of A. G. Gaston.*

Although the heyday of the Fourth Avenue District ended along with the Jim Crow era, its historical significance is recognized by National Park Service designations. Among the notable buildings in the district are the A. G. Gaston Motel, as well as two designed by well-known Black architects, the Prince Hall Grand Lodge and the 16th Street Baptist Church.

On September 15, 1963, the 16th Street Baptist Church was bombed, killing four young girls. Today, a statue of Martin Luther King Jr. watches over the church.

CHAPTER 4

Allensworth, California

Fourth Avenue and Sweet Auburn were districts within towns. However, Allensworth, California, was an entire city designed, financed, built, and governed by Black Americans. Allen Allensworth began his life getting punished for learning to read and write, but he went on to create the town of Allensworth.

Allensworth was a town of both farmers and retailers. In 1908 Allen Allensworth recruited Black people to come to California and build businesses. The trip west was long and full of danger, and some didn't survive it. Those who did found a well-governed haven away from the segregation worries of the South. Farming, shops, and restaurants were all profitable. Most important, the members of the Allensworth community valued education and built their own school from community-donated funds. A yearly June graduation was one of

Allensworth's major community celebrations.
Allensworth even became its own judiciary district. Its
citizens elected their own judge who held court when
people disagreed or got into trouble.

Allensworth was born into enslavement. He escaped captivity during
the Civil War and later became a soldier for the Union army.

Unfortunately, Allensworth's success was short-lived. After Allen Allensworth died tragically in 1914, water delivery problems made life in Allensworth difficult. Further, the men in town had to leave to fight in World War I (1914–1918). Still, Allensworth is famous as the only city in California to be planned, designed, financed, and governed by Black Americans.

Today, Allensworth is partially preserved at the Colonel Allensworth

CHAPTER 5

Black Wall Street, Tulsa, Oklahoma

One of the most famous communities known for Black achievement and wealth was Greenwood in Tulsa, Oklahoma. The most well known of the Black financial districts, nicknamed "Black Wall Street," the community attracted many Black people. They were looking to make a better life in a community that offered some relief from racism. In the early 1900s, O. W. Gurley, a teacher, politician, and landowner, planned a community he called Greenwood. Blacks seeking opportunity came to Greenwood and built businesses of all kinds. Black people could get whatever they needed, from construction materials to groceries to luxury salon treatments. Like in other wealthy Black communities, there were restaurants, theaters, and luxury hotels. Community members could depend on each other for news, entertainment, medical treatment, and all types of goods and services.

In 1921 a group of Black men from Greenwood organized to prevent a Black man who had been wrongfully accused and was awaiting trial from being **lynched** before he was tried. The White men were angry at not being able to carry out their lynching plan. In retaliation, they burned Greenwood. The massacre killed an estimated 150 to 300 people and left 10,000 others homeless.

Unlike many other communities, however, Greenwood's reign as one of the wealthiest Black communities didn't end because of desegregation. An angry mob of White people used airplanes and firebombs to burn it down.

In 2021, President Joe Biden traveled to Tulsa to commemorate and grieve with the Tulsa community on the 100th anniversary of the Tulsa Massacre. This recognition marks a turning point in the way people learn about historical violence against Black communities.

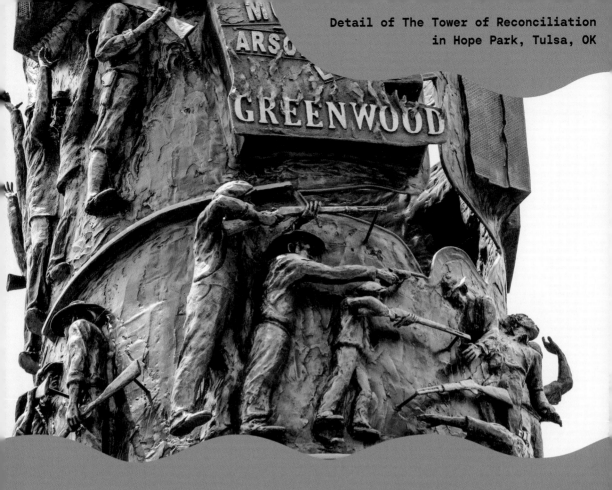

Tulsa's Black Wall Street, New York's Harlem, and the other communities mentioned are only a few of the Black communities that prospered during segregation. Houston's Third Ward, North Carolina's Hayti District, U Street in Washington, D.C., Virginia's Jackson Ward, and California's West Oakland are all examples of the spirit and drive that led Black people to build wealth in spite of the challenges of racism and segregation. By studying the histories of these vibrant communities, we can help our country continue to close wealth gaps that exist today.

CHAPTER 6

Black Wealth in the United States Today

Although Black communities in the United States still face challenges in creating, maintaining, and passing down wealth to their children, there are those who overcome those challenges. The country is home to both Black billionaires and Black wealthy neighborhoods.

Laws existed throughout most of the 20th century that prevented equal access to property ownership for Black people. Because of those laws, people in Black communities have not always had the chance to buy houses or land. Buying a home is one of the main ways families build wealth. Only recently have young Black home buyers begun to be able to buy property when and where they choose to.

Redlining was a process of refusing financial services to people based on where they lived. This was used as a way to refuse loans and insurance to Black people.

Although less strictly segregated than in the past, enclaves still exist. For example, many Black celebrities live in the Ladera Heights, Baldwin Hills, and "Black Hollywood" neighborhoods in California. In Maryland, Black professionals flock to several predominantly Black neighborhoods in Prince Georges County. Throughout the nation and the world, wherever there is wealth, there is Black wealth. That achievement is a testament to the communities, business owners, professionals, entertainers, athletes, educators, politicians, and hardworking people who paved the way.

Black wealth and success is everywhere!

Making a Way Out of NO WAY!!!

Journaling Your Way to Justice!

Have you ever heard of a vision board? People create vision boards to set goals for their future. You can do the same thing by creating a Justice Journal! In your Justice Journal, you can write your way to a better future for everyone.

Start by taking a notebook and adding things to the cover that represent the kind of world you want to see. You can use magazine clippings, crayons, markers, colored pencils, or words. Just be creative in designing your Justice Journal. It's a place where you will write about the world you want to see and then make a plan to create it!

As we have learned, Black people have made significant contributions in their communities in the face of adversity. When they were not permitted to live in certain neighborhoods or work at certain places because of the color of their skin, they built their own wealth and communities. They made a way out of no way.

If you could build any kind of community, what would it be? Who would live there? What would it look like? Where would it be?

Write or draw in your Justice Journal and create a vision for your community. Dream big!!!

EXTEND YOUR LEARNING

WEBSITE

Visit *https://blog.rhinoafrica.com/2018/03/27/9-ancient-african-kingdoms/* to learn about Black wealth before colonization.

BOOKS

Bolden, Tonya. *Searching for Sarah Rector: The Richest Black Girl in America.* New York, NY: Abrams Books for Young Readers, 2014.

Feldman, Lynne B. *A Sense of Place: Birmingham's Black Middle-Class Community*, 1890–1930. Tuscaloosa, AL: University of Alabama Press, 1999.

Meyer, Carolyn. *White Lilacs.* Orlando, FL: Harcourt, 2007.

GLOSSARY

enslavement (in-SLAYV-muhnt) the process of forcing people to work without pay and treating them like property; many Black people were enslaved throughout the world in the past

colonization (kah-luh-nuh-ZAY-shuhn) the act of people from one country going into another country to gain control of the resources or the people of that country

desegregation (dee-seh-gruh-GAY-shuhn) the elimination of laws and customs like Black Codes that maintained U.S. apartheid between 1865 and 1965

enclaves (EHN-klayvs) social units where people who are socially similar gather by choice

entrepreneurs (ahn-truh-pruh-NUHRS) people who start their own businesses

freedman (FREED-muhn) a person freed from enslavement

gospel (GAH-spuhl) a genre of Christian music from the Black church that traces its roots to spirituals, field songs, blues, and ragtime

Great Migration (GRAYT mye-GRAY-shuhn) the journey of millions of freed Black people to the U.S. North, Midwest, and West after slavery ended

jazz (JAZ) traditional music artform developed by Black Americans that relies heavily on improvisation

Jim Crow laws (JIM KROH LAWZ) a series of laws common between 1865 and 1965 that kept freed Black people from full rights of U.S. citizenship; also known as Black Codes

Ku Klux Klan (KOO KLUHKS KLAN) a violent hate group founded to prevent Black people from gaining full rights of U.S. citizenship

lynched (LINCH-duh) having killed an accused person without a trial; lynchings were often carried out by mobs

segregation (seh-grih-GAY-shuhn) legal separation of Black and white citizens in public places such as restaurants, schools, and parks; also known as apartheid

wealth gaps (WELTH GAPZ) financial distances between the rich and poor; wealth gaps in the United States are larger than in any other major developed country

INDEX